Julius Goebel

Poetry in the Limburger Chronik

Julius Goebel

Poetry in the Limburger Chronik

ISBN/EAN: 9783743349827

Manufactured in Europe, USA, Canada, Australia, Japa

Cover: Foto ©ninafisch / pixelio.de

Manufactured and distributed by brebook publishing software
(www.brebook.com)

Julius Goebel

Poetry in the Limburger Chronik

Poetry in the Limburger Chronik.

BY

DR. JULIUS GOEBEL,

JOHNS HOPKINS UNIVERSITY.

[Reprinted from THE AMERICAN JOURNAL OF PHILOLOGY.]

BALTIMORE:
PRESS OF ISAAC FRIEDENWALD
1888.

[Reprinted from AMERICAN JOURNAL OF PHILOLOGY, Vol. VIII, No. 2.]

II.—POETRY IN THE LIMBURGER CHRONIK.

I.

Travelling through the romantic valley of the Lahn, we meet about half way between Wetzlar and the Rhein the beautiful ancient city of Limburg. Situated in one of the most fertile parts of Germany, commonly called "der goldne Grund," and chiefly inhabited by a Catholic population, the city with its surroundings, especially during festive days, still bears a mediaeval appearance. Its cathedral, with an abbey founded in the tenth century, belongs to the master-works of the thirteenth century, and is said to contain the tomb of the German emperor, Conrad I, who died in 918. Limburg, however, has become still more celebrated in the history of German literature by reason of the chronicle which was written there in the latter part of the fourteenth century.

Not only containing numerous accounts of events which are of great value for the local history of the city and the bordering principalities, but also giving highly interesting descriptions of the costumes, as well as the manners and customs of the fourteenth century, of music and painting, and, above all, preserving many songs of that period, our chronicle must very early have enjoyed a great popularity, as we may see from the number of manuscripts in which it is preserved to us. When later, during the time of the Reformation and under the influence of the humanists, an interest in the study of German antiquities was awakened, a rich patrician of Frankfort-a-M., Johann Friedrich Faust, for the first time published it in 1617. Two years later a second edition was necessary. This edition, brought out under the unsuitable name of "Fasti Limburgenses," has, in spite of its many defects, until recently been the main source of information concerning the chronicle. The succeeding generation, having lost through the Thirty Years War its national self-consciousness, did not know how to appreciate the value of the book. One editor, in 1747, even complains: "dass der Historicus sich hie und dort mit Kleinigkeiten aufhalte, zum Exempel mit der Kleider-Mode, mit der Witterung, mit einfältigen Liedgern."

The two great reformers of German literature, Lessing and Herder, with their keen eye for the poetical element and their deep historical predilections, again called attention to this important document of the fourteenth century. Thus we find in Lessing's posthumous works,[1] under the chapter Beiträge zur Geschichte der deutschen Sprache und Literatur von den Minnesängern bis auf Luthern 1777, numerous extracts from the chronicle, which he characterizes with the following words : " Es ist die älteste deutsche Chronik, so viel ich weiss, äusserst merkwürdig, weil sie so viele besondere Kleinigkeiten mitnimmt, dass sie auch fleissig der Lieder gedenkt, die jedes Jahr am meisten gesungen wurden, und sie also noch oft von mir wird angeführt werden müssen."

Herder's opinion of the value of the Limburger Chronik was so high that he intended to give long extracts from it at the beginning of the third book of his celebrated Volkslieder.[2] Seeing, however, that it would take too much space, he quotes only a few sentences from it, finally giving its whole title, and expressing the wish that some one else would make proper use of it. His advice has not been followed. While some collectors of popular poetry like Uhland, Erk, Böhme and others, inserted one or two of the songs into their collections, the fame of our chronicle really rested on a few scanty and, for the most part, erroneous remarks in our histories of German literature. The principal reason for this lack of attention may, perhaps, be found in the want of a critical edition ; for, strange to say, until 1883 we had nothing but a careless reprint of the imperfect edition of Faust. We owe it to the diligent research of Arthur Wyss that we now possess an excellent edition of the chronicle in the Monumenta Germaniae Historica. In his little treatise " Die Limburger Chronik untersucht von Arthur Wyss," he, for the first time, inquires into the relation of the different MSS, at the same time settling the question as to the authorship of our document. The results of his investigations being reinforced by fortunate discoveries, were afterwards embodied in his large edition just named.

An inquiry into the nature of the poetry contained in the Limburger Chronik, its origin, and its relation to former and later lyrics, may be justified by various reasons. While the student will perhaps welcome a handy collection of the songs interspersed in the Chronik which he now can only find in the insufficient form of Faust's text, made by a dilettante musician in the Jahrbuch für

[1] Lessing, ed. Lachmann, XI 468.　　[2] Herder, ed. Suphan, XXV 320, 459.

musikalische Wissenschaft,[1] he will probably also wish for a critical text. For Arthur Wyss, in his laudable effort to give, by the aid of certain documents, the original form of the chronicle, has frequently, for the sake of a " normalisirte Text," reconstructed the language, not always to the advantage of the poems. The principal aim of this paper, however, will be to inquire whether the poetry in our chronicle is " Volkspoesie," or whether it belongs to the declining " Minnepoesie " or the rising " Meistergesang." A very interesting and lively discussion as to the age of lyrical Volkspoesie, which, of course, would also affect other forms of poetry, has recently been carried on, growing out of certain views of Wilmanns.[2] Starting from the fact that documents from the time before 1160 are wanting, he has denied the existence of any such poetry previous to that year. Burdach[3] and Richard M. Meyer[4] have tried to controvert this opinion by the use of various arguments, without appealing, however, to the songs in the Limburger Chronik. Now, could it be proved that the poetry which has been handed down to us in our chronicle was in no way influenced by the development of artistic lyrical poetry in the thirteenth century, could we further show that a close relation exists between the contents, the metrical forms, the poetical expressions, etc., of our songs and the beginnings of the Minnepoesie as represented in "Minnesangs Frühling" as well as in the Volkslieder of the fifteenth and sixteenth centuries, then I believe we shall be justified in drawing a conclusion as to the age of German Volkspoesie in general.

To this end it does not suffice that we have the assurance of the author of our Chronik : "item zu diser zit da sang und pfeif man dit lit overalle," or "in allen Duschen landen."

It is necessary to fix the position and character of the Limburger Chronik among similar documents of the time, and to ascertain, above all, whether its author probably composed the songs himself while in his poetical vanity he gave them the attribute of popularity.

The Chronicle of Limburg belongs to that class of historical literature which had a rich development at the close of the thirteenth and during the fourteenth century, owing to a deeper and more widespread interest in historical matters as it is found especially among the citizens of the great German cities.[5] They

[1] I 115.   [2] Wilmanns, Leben Walthers v. d. Vogelw. 16.
[3] Zeitsch. f. d. A. XXVII 343 ff.   [4] Ibid. XXIX 121 ff.
[5] Cf. O. Lorenz, Deutschlands Geschichtsquellen im Mittelalter. Wattenbach, Geschichtsquellen.

are not men of broad views and profound learning, like the historians in the times of the Hohenstaufen, who now try to supply the demand of readers. Recruiting their ranks mostly from the lower nobility, from the citizens and the clergy, they make it their chief object to be popular. And corresponding with the course of German politics, with the decline of imperial power and the rise of territorial interests, we find that most of these historical documents are local histories, chronicles of cities. At that time we scarcely meet with an attempt to write a general history of the world or to penetrate by deeper reasoning the course of historical events. But while they betray a charming naïveté in the absence of thoughts, these chroniclers cannot be called free from certain *motifs*. Historical legends, which to a great extent form the charm of the earlier historians, are almost entirely wanting, and whenever they are introduced, it is done, not with the naïve credulity of earlier centuries, but with the consciousness of an intention to produce certain effects. Being thus the representatives of a very prosaic view of the world, they did well to choose the form of prose for their productions, for they are intolerable as soon as they try to become poetical. But as writers of German prose, which assured them great popularity, they deserve a high place in the history of German literature. The great development of almost all poetical forms during the twelfth and thirteenth centuries scarcely left space for the use of prose as it had been cultivated in the latter part of the tenth century in the monastery of St. Gall. It was relegated to the position of the sole medium of expression of theological literature, for the popular form of sermons, or the more scientific writings which contain the philosophical speculations of the mystics. A close relation between the language of bodies of laws like the " Sachsenspiegel " and " Schwabenspiegel " may also be observed.

The gradual turning toward a more prosaic view of the world, the favored use of popular German prose, and the awakening interest in historical studies are principally due, however, to the two great orders, the Franciscans and Dominicans. It was only natural that the Church should start a movement of reaction against the spirit of a time which resembles very much that of the classical times of Lessing, Kant, Goethe and Schiller. Poetry which, to the middle of the eleventh century, had been cultivated almost exclusively by the clergy, had become an ethical power in the hands of knights and burghers. Their ideals were independent of those of the Church, they preached religious tolerance, and in Walther von der Vogelweide the Pope had one of his most dangerous enemies. As the great mass of the German clergy had no influence upon their own people, the Pope in his reactionary efforts very prudently made use of those orders, whose original purpose was the conversion of heretics not only in South France but also in Germany. For here, too, the belief of the Church had been dangerously shaken, and stories of saints and miracles found no believers, according to a contemporary, unless the preacher added carefully the exact place and time where such miraculous occurrences had taken place. It seems that clerical astuteness speedily took this practical hint, and we soon see them collecting accounts of all kinds of events, historical and miraculous, thus producing an endless literature of more or less value. The Franciscans, who gave Germany some of its greatest preachers, made these collections mostly for practical homiletic use; they were the arsenals from which the monks took arms for attacking the gay, worldly life in the castles, the cities and the country. The Dominicans, on the other hand, who, from the beginning, show more scientific tendencies, manifest the same spirit in their treatment of history. The order which produced scholastics like Albertus Magnus, the celebrated teacher of Thomas Aquinas, of whom jealous Franciscans said, "Albertus ex asino factus est philosophus et ex philosopho asinus"—the same order created a rich historical literature bearing the character of compilations like many of their theological works. Like the Franciscans they either wrote themselves chronicles of cities, or persuaded others to do so. A brief sketch of the literary life and the tendencies of these orders was necessary in order to characterize the author of our chronicle, who, as we shall find, also belonged to the clergy.

Various accounts of the authorship of the Chronicle of Limburg were given by the different publishers, until Arthur Wyss, in his excellent little treatise, proved beyond doubt that it was written by Tilemann Elhem von Wolfhagen. From several documents recently reprinted in Wyss's large edition of our chronicle, it appears that Tilemann was town clerk of the city of Limburg from 1370–98. From the same source we learn that he belonged to the diocese of Treves. Wolfhagen, therefore, a village not far from Cassel, is evidently his native place, and he was born there probably about the year 1347; for, in chapter 13 of the chronicle, he says, "You shall know, everything that happened between 1347 and 1402 has happened in my days, and I have through God's help seen it with my eyes and heard from my childhood until now." Although an ecclesiastic brought up in one of the monastic schools of Maintz, he calls himself in the barbarous Latin of his time *clericus uxoratus*, the name of his wife being Grede. It is evident, therefore, that he was not an ordained priest, but had changed his original calling to that of an imperial notary and town clerk of Limburg.

Much more than these few scanty notes upon his life, however, may be gained from Tilemann's work, in order to draw a picture of the man. Frequent quotations from Aristotle, Cato, the Corpus Juris and the Bible show that he was a man well trained in the scholastic learning of his time. His mention of Johannes Buridan (1327-50), the pupil of Occam and inventor of the "ass between two bundles of hay," probably serves to show that Tilemann, for a time at least, had studied under the great philosopher in Paris. Remembering the picture of the theological world of his time, the motives and efforts of the Dominicans and Franciscans, we must, however, say that Tilemann represents a great exception. While he shares their interest in the writing of history, while he still feels himself an ecclesiastic and condemns certain heretical movements as directed against the Church and the Pope, he does not share their fanatic hatred of poetry and worldly education. Nowhere in the chronicle do we find even a trace that he was led by theological motives or followed the tendencies of the other chroniclers, and only from a few passages can we infer that he consulted other historical sources.

He relates, according to his own confession, what he has seen and heard; the contents of the chronicle are, therefore, taken from life, and to this it owes its lasting charm. We hear not only of lesser or greater political events, but he tells us also of the weather in different years, the harvest, the quality of the wine, and of abnormal births. From him we learn of one of the first historical strikes, of social and religious movements; and to him we owe most valuable accounts of important paintings, as well as of the costumes not only of men but also of women—for he was a married man. His principal interest, however, seems to have been concentrated upon the arts of music and poetry. And while we may safely conclude that a man of such wide interests, that such a keen and faithful observer, can never have gone through the school of one of the fanatical orders above mentioned, but rather belongs to the old conservative class of ecclesiastics who joined the knights and citizens in their gay, poetic life, we must still ask how it is possible to meet with such a unique personality in this century? Comparing other chronicles with a view to the poetry which they contain, we frequently find songs scattered here and there, but they are always chosen to serve some purpose of the author; they are introduced mostly as stylistic embellishments. Tilemann's collection, on the other hand, appears to have been made entirely for its own sake, and, furthermore, betrays so much intimate knowledge of poetry and music as an art that we cannot help supposing that its author was either an exceptionally highly educated amateur or a poet himself, probably belonging to the newly arising school of mastersingers. We know that in Maintz there existed one of the first of these schools, which showed, according to a contemporary (cf. Germ. XV 200), a decidedly conservative spirit, in opposition to the newly invented measures and melodies of other schools. Is it not possible that Tilemann, besides receiving his theological training in Maintz, may also have acquired the poetical education of that mastersinger school? A close examination of his style and of those poetical passages which doubtless belong to him, will perhaps give us a satisfactory answer.

It cannot be denied that Tilemann's style, although keeping within the typical forms of such chronicles, is remarkably German in its character, and free from the influence of Latin style which has continued to corrupt German prose down to our own time. The tranquillity of epic objectiveness is spread over the chronicle in general, and several descriptions of persons might find a place in any great epic poem. Relating the contest which the city of Limburg had with the Knight Cune, *i. e.* Konrad von Falkenstein, the protector of Maintz and Treves, he describes him in the following manner: " Item nu saltu wissen phyzonomien unde gestalt hern Conen vurgenant, want ich in dicke gesehen unde geprufet han in sime wesen unde in mancher siner manirunge. He was ein herlich stark man von libe unde wol gepersoniret unde gross von allem gelune, unde hatte ein gross heupt mit eime struben widem brunen krulle, ein breit antlitze mit pussenden backen, ein sharp menlich gesichte, einen bescheiden mont mit glefsen etzlicher masse dicke ; die nase was breit, mit gerumeden naselochern, die nase was ime mitten nider gedrucket; mit eime grossen kinne unde mit einer hohen stirne, unde hatte auch ein gross brost unde rodelfare under sinen augen, unde stont uf sinen beinen als ein lewe, unde hatte gutliche geberde gen sinen frunden, unde wanne dass he zornig was, so

pusseden unde floderten ime sinc backen unde stonden ime
herlichen unde wislichen unde nit obel."

While Tilemann shows in passages like this that he had certain
poetical gifts, he does not betray the same faculty in his verses.
The latter are, with one exception, translations of quotations from
the Bible and ancient writers, and appear to be made according to
the prescription, " Reim' dich oder ich fress' Dich." Thus he
translates a sentence of Aristotle : "Amicus est consolativus amico
visione et sermone: Ein frunt sal sime frunde trostlich sin unde
dun dass mit rede und gesicht shin." Speaking of the locusts
which appeared in Germany in 1362 and did great damage, he
quotes the 46th verse of the LXXVII psalm, " Et dedit erugini
fructus eorum et laborum eorum locustis," and translates : " Di
rupen sollent ire fruchte leben, arbeit der lute ist den Haun-
schrecken gegeben."

Indeed, such verses may pass for the poetical pastime of an
amateur who is trying his skill in hours of leisure, but nobody will
find in them the traces of a poetical genius. And even at a more
important occasion, when Tilemann evidently is so deeply agitated
that he asks his readers to pray to God for him, and his local
patriotism takes the form of poetry, his verses do not rise above
the level of rhymed prose. The independence of Limburg had
been at stake after the death of the princes of Limburg, and the
Archbishop of Treves, in whose diocese the city was situated,
came with many knights and soldiers in order to take possession.
Before doing this, however, he called the city council together and
asked them what rights and privileges the Archbishop might,
in their opinion, claim. But instead of being frightened, the
head of the council, the burgomaster Boppe, gave such sharp
and legal answers that the Archbishop was astonished, and
refrained from touching the independence of Limburg. Full of
joy and just pride, Tilemann then writes the following lines :

" Daran gedenket, it jungen unde ir alden
dass ir mit wisheit moget behalden
uwer lip, gut unde ere
dass ist uwern kinden gute mere."

It would certainly be a charitable injustice towards Tilemann
were we, after having examined the poetry which he claims as his
own, to suspect him of having written any of the beautiful songs
occurring in the latter part of the chronicle. There is every reason
for believing that he is not the composer of any one of the songs

which he tells us were so popular, at various times, in Germany. Nor do passages in which he shows his knowledge of the technical language of the mastersingers prove, as we shall see later when we treat of the metrical peculiarities of these poems, that he must have practised the art of poetry to any further extent than that which has been indicated above.

Looking over the whole collection of poems contained in the Chronicle of Limburg, we may divide it into three different classes : (1) Poetry showing the influence of the declining Minnepoesie ; (2) Religious poetry ; (3) Popular songs.

There is only one poem in the chronicle which strictly belongs to the first class, and which bears the name of its author, Herr Reinhard von Westerburg.

This knight frequently appears in historical documents of that time, not only figuring in many of those fights in which the lesser knights constantly indulged, but also as a favored follower of Emperor Ludwig of Bavaria. He also must have enjoyed great fame as a poet, besides being a very jovial, witty and wild fellow. We possess a beautiful characterization of him by one of his con- temporaries, contained in a poem of a MS of the fifteenth century, which was formerly in the possession of W. Grimm, and is now to be found in the Royal Library of Berlin (cf. Zeitschrift f. d. A. XIII 366 ff.). The author of this poem represents himself as walking in the woods, where he finds an elderly but still handsome lady. As she does not answer his greeting, he takes her by the hand, whereupon she tells him that thirty years ago she had founded a school for the purpose of teaching young knights the rules of honor and drawing them from the pool of disgrace. Tired of the great mass of knights, she had selected from their numbers twelve who had now developed into the bloom of knighthood and were ready to be dismissed, and she herself needed rest. Here the poet interrupts her, and proposes that she should continue her school. She asks him to name some knights whom she might take. This he does, but when mentioning Reinhard von Westerburg he cautiously adds, " He is a little wild and needs your training."

The story which Tilemann relates is entirely in accordance with this, and furnishes a delightful illustration of Reinhard's wildness. He says : " Item da man schreip dusent druhundert unde siben unde vierzig jar, da worden di von Cobelenze jemerlichen irslagen unde nider geworfen bi Grensauwe unde bliben ir doit hundert unde zwene unde sibenzig man unde worden ir auch darzu vil gefangen unde dass det Reinhart, herre zu Westerburg. Unde der selbe Reinhart was gar ein kluger ritter von libe, von sinne unde von gestalt, unde reit keiser Ludewigen ser nach unde sang unde machte he dit lit :

> ' Ob ich durch si den hals zubreche,
> wer reche mir den schaiden dan ?
> so enhette ich nimans der mich reche ;
> ich bin ein ungefrunter man.
> Darumb so muss ich selber warten,
> wi ez mir gelegen si.
> Ich enhan nit trostes von der zarten,
> si ist irs gemudes fri.
> Wel si min nit, di werde reine,
> so muss ich wol orlaup han.
> Uf ir genade achte ich kleine,
> sich, daz lasse ich si vurstan.'

Da der vurgenant keiser Ludewig daz lit gehorte, darumb so strafte he den herren von Westerburg unde saide, he wolde ez der frouwen gebessert haben. Da nam der herre von Westerburg eine kurze zit unde saide, he wolde den frauwen hesseren unde sang daz lit :

> ' In jammers noden ich gar vurdreven bin
> durch ein wif so minnecliche,' etc.

Da sprach Keiser Ludewig: 'Westerburg, du hast uns nu wol gebessert.' "

It is evident that Reinhard's poem belongs to that healthy opposition which seems to have begun even in the time of Walther v. d. Vogelweide, and which is generally called the decline of Minnepoesie. The conditions upon which the latter was based were too unnatural, the circles in which it moved too narrow, to assure it a longer life. For that sickly romantic admiration until recently prevailing in Germany and elsewhere, which saw in those knights the true representatives of *die gute, alte Zeit,* and adored them as the incarnation of *Zucht und Ehrbarkeit,* has fortunately passed away. While we fully acknowledge the beauties of many of their productions, we cannot help seeing in their constant groaning, whining and lamenting something extremely unknightly, especially as it was meant for married women, and had but one aim in view, the immorality of which cannot be denied, even if we call it, in Walther's elegant language, "halsen triuten bigelegen." The opposition, however, was not caused by such ethical considerations. Very soon the more sensible minds began to see the comical element in the relation between knight and lady; above all, they began to feel that the fundamental idea upon which the whole nature of Minnepoesie rested was as unnatural as it was wrong. The idea that man is the servant of woman had not grown upon German soil, and in spite of all apparent flatteries, contained a very low conception of the woman, if we remember the real aim of this servitude.

It is very interesting to follow the development of the opposition, a history of which we do not yet possess. Very significantly, it is inaugurated by that poet in whom the sensual element of Minnepoesie reached its climax, and who afterwards became for this reason the hero of a popular legend, by Tannhäuser. He ridicules Minnepoesie by enumerating impossible things which the lady in whose "service" he is, required of him. And as he already praises the simple peasant girl whose love is won more easily than that of a lady in the higher circles, Neidhard von Reuenthal makes the villages near Vienna the scene of his love adventures, and while preserving the air of a minnesinger, brings about highly ludicrous situations. Their followers, Steinmar, Gottfried von Neifen and others go still further by scorning the unnatural feeling itself. Steinmar even compares the throbbing of his love-sick heart to the jumping of a pig in a bag (Als ein swîn in einem sacke vert mîn herze hin und dar). But I have searched in vain in the minnesingers of that period to find a single example in which the poet addressed his ridicule to the lady herself as Reinhard von Westerburg does here. The ties of etiquette and tradition requiring the highest respect for the lady, were too strong yet, even at this late period, and it was because Tilemann felt them to be broken that he mentioned Reinhard's poem. This offence against tradition, which really meant the dissolution of the whole fabric on Minnepoetry, was felt still more keenly by the representative of conservatism, whose glory was based upon the splendor of knighthood by the emperor. For this reason he reprimands Reinhard, asking him to turn from his former course; and for this reason Reinhard assumes the old, worn-out, love-sick attitude of a minnesinger, behind which we can after all not help seeing the wild rogue.

Of the same importance which Reinhard's poem has for the history of Minnepoetry are Tilemann's accounts of the development of religious poetry. The same clear, observing mind which, either by instinctive interest or from scientific motives, noted a

most valuable turn in secular poetic art, has preserved us also an
interesting source of knowledge in the field of sacred hymnology.
Through Hoffmann von Fallersleben's diligent researches we
know that the German church hymn is not entirely a new creation
of Luther's.[1] Long before him the German spirit had revolted
against the stupid inactivity with which Roman priests and the
Roman liturgy had oppressed it. We can trace how the people,
beginning with a few senseless vowels added to the strange *Kyrie
eleison*, which they were allowed to sing, gradually created a
German church hymn, much to the dislike of the Roman clergy.
We owe it to the hate and persecutions of the latter that most of
these songs were lost. The few which we still possess of the
twelfth, thirteenth and fourteenth centuries, especially those
addressed to the Virgin Mary, are filled with the deepest and most
sublime religious feeling, and some songs which the people sang
at Easter and Pentecost, such as "Christ ist erstanden" and
" Komm, heilger Geist," are still jewels of our present hymnals.
Religious sects especially, as e. g. the mystics, which developed
a highly spiritual life, cultivated religious poetry, and thus we find
that the specimens preserved by Tilemann also belong to one of
the religious movements of the fourteenth century. For, excepting
the century of the Reformation, no other period was so deeply
agitated by religion as the fourteenth century; and in many
respects it may be compared to our present time. Not only do
we find there the first beginning of great socialistic movements in
Germany, but we also meet with the mania of our own time as
well, the 'Antisemitentum,' the 'Judenhetze,' and even with the
premonition of our Salvation Army, the Flagellants, among whom
originated the songs of which we are about to treat.

Owing to the few and, for the most part, very imperfect and
prejudiced sources of information afforded by contemporary
writers, our knowledge of the whole movement is extremely
limited. Although it has been proved by Haeser (" Lehrbuch der
Gesch. der Medicin") and Hecker ("Die grossen Volkskrank-
heiten des Mittelalters") that this movement was caused by the
so-called Black Death, mainly a disease of the lungs, which had
been imported from Asia, and which swept through Europe from
the Black Sea to Spain, devouring millions of people, we do not
know its exact connection with the persecution of the Jews and

[1] Hoffmann von Fallersleben, Geschichte des deutschen Kirchenliedes bis
auf Luthers Zeit.

the geographical route of the Flagellants. Recent investigation, however, has shown that the order of events which is usually accepted, viz., Black Death—Persecution of the Jews—Flagellants, has to be changed, for Germany at least, into Persecution of the Jews—Flagellants—Black Death.[1] The news of the approaching plague was a welcome pretext for getting rid of the Jews, who, as Roscher ("Ansichten der Volkswirtschaft") has proved, were hated as the possessors of money and as public extortioners. Malice, stupidity and religious fanaticism manufactured the story that they had poisoned the wells, and in less than one year all the Jews scattered from Cologne to Austria were killed. The words 'Juden- mord,' 'Judenbrand,' 'Judenschlacht' are technical terms in the chronicles, which find it quite natural that in Strassburg 2000 Jews were burned at one time *ad maiorem Dei gloriam.* One chroni- cler remarks (Diessenhofen) *crederem finem Hebreorum advenisse,* while another writer coolly concludes *requiescant in inferno* (Chronicum Lampetrinum). We have sufficient proof that the Flagellants, who appear simultaneously with these persecutions, frequently instigated them in the places at which they arrived with their processions.

Two great periods are to be distinguished in the history of this peculiar fanatical movement. Driven by an agonizing fear of the approaching death, which no human art or power could stay, superstitious people, seeing the wrath and judgment of God in the pest, organized in different parts of Germany a religious order composed of those who thought to be able to reconcile the wrath of God by punishing and torturing themselves. The impression which they created wherever they appeared was overpowering and heartrending, for a genuine religious enthusiasm seemed to break forth like a revelation from mysterious depths. As Tilemann reports, knights, citizens and peasants joined the new order. Closener, the chronicler of Strassburg, writes: "Whenever the Flagellants scourged themselves, then the greatest crowds assem- bled and the greatest weeping was to be witnessed, for they believed everything to be true." And another writer, Hervord, says : *Cor lapideum esset quod talia sine lacrimis posset accipere.* It was in this first time, when they were welcomed everywhere and still filled with the spirit of repentance, that our hymns were composed.

Soon, however, we notice a great change in public opinion as

[1] R. Hoeniger, Der schwarze Tod in Deutschland.

well as among the Flagellants themselves. Notwithstanding all the praying, singing and scourging, the plague appeared and swept away millions and millions of people. We must not be surprised that the belief of the public was shaken, that it began to look upon the whole spectacle as a pious fraud. The Flagellants themselves seem to have felt their failing, and in order to preserve themselves they directed their agitation against the clergy, for they were sure this would not fail to make them popular. For a time it seems as if they had successfully calculated upon the public hatred of the depraved clergy. The movement assumes immense proportions ; it spreads over all Germany; even women and children become Flagellants. Again they are seen to change their policy. Having filled their ranks with the outcasts of society, they begin to show socialistic and anarchical tendencies. Long before they had ceased to be an element of great ethical strength and influence. While in the earlier period their members had not dared to speak to women, a chronicler now writes: *transiverunt eciam in similibus turmis mulieres et virgines que, sicut audivi, nonnuncquam plenis, salva reverencia, gremiis redierunt*, thus also foreshadowing the frequent elopements of our Salvation Army. They caused a second general persecution of the Jews; they entered and pillaged villages and cities, and finally threatened a complete overthrow of society. A final and radical change in public opinion now follows. Papal and imperial power unite for their destruction. In the same dry words with which the chroniclers spoke of the burning of the Jews they now relate the general slaughter of the Flagellants.

It is another proof of the impartiality of Tilemann that, although he shared the popular condemnation of the Flagellants, he has nevertheless written an accurate account of their first appearance.

We fortunately possess another description of the movement, entirely independent from Tilemann's, which not only verifies the statements of the latter, but will also assist us in obtaining a clear picture of all the ceremonies and processions accompanied by the singing of hymns. It was written by Fritsche (Friedrich) Closener, a contemporary of Tilemann living in Strassburg, and likewise an ecclesiastic and chronicler of his native city.[1] The Flagellants generally marched in troops consisting of one to three hundred members, who had pledged themselves, before entering the brother-

---

[1] Cf. Lorenz, Geschichtsquellen, p. 33; K. Hegel, Die Chroniken der deutschen Städte, Vol. 8, p. 3 (Einleitung).

hood, to observe strictly its regulations during the thirty to thirty-four days of the procession. As soon as they approached a city or a village they formed a line, following two by two the bearers of precious silk and velvet flags. They were clad in very plain clothes; upon their cloaks and hats red crosses were fastened. And while the church bells were rung to greet them, they marched to the church singing, according to Tilemann's version, the following song:

> Ist dise bedefart so here
> Crist fur selber zu Jherusalem
> und furte ein cruze in siner hant.
> Nu helf uns der heilant!

As Tilemann relates, the hymn had been composed for this special purpose, and was used in later times during the processions, "wanne man di heiligen treit." It has been preserved by 'Closener[1] in a more perfect form, and it is interesting to observe in this song, as well as in the others recorded by Closener, the constant changes which every genuine folksong has to undergo.

> Nû ist die bettevart sô hêr
> Crist reit selber gen Jherusalem;
> er fûrt ein krütze an sîner hant.
> nû helf uns der heilant!

> Nû ist die bettevart sô guot.
> hilf uns, herre, durch dîn heiliges bluot,
> daz du an dem krütze vergossen hast,
> und uns in dem ellende gelossen hast.

> Nû ist die strôsze alsô breit
> die uns zu unsere lieben frowen treit
> in unsere lieben frowen lant.
> nû helfe uns der heilant!

> Wir sullent die busze an uns nemen,
> daz wir gote deste bas gezemen
> aldort in sînes vatters rîch.
> des bitten wir dich sünder alle gelîch.
>   so bitten wir den vil heiligen Crist
>   der alle der welte gewaltig ist.

As soon as they had entered the church they kneeled down and sang:

> Jhesus wart gelabet mit gallen
> des sollen wir an sin cruze vallen. (Tilemann.)

[1] Cf. K. Hegel, Chroniken, VIII 105; L. Uhland, Volkslieder, II 824; W. Wackernagel, Lesebuch, I 1246.

Then they threw themselves on the ground, stretching out their arms in the form of a cross. In this position they remained until their precentor sang :

> Nû hebent ûf die ûwern hende
> daz got dis grosze sterben wende. (Closener.)

After the first part of their exercises was thus ended, the inhabitants of the city or village invited them home and "büttentz in wol" (fed them). The principal performance, the scourging, generally took place twice a day either in a churchyard or in some large open place. Thither they marched in the same order in which they had entered the church, formed a circle, took off their shoes and uncovered the upper part of their bodies. Hereupon they lay down on the ground, indicating by their positions the different sins which they had committed. The adulterer, e. g. placed himself on his face, the murderer on his back, the perjurer held up three fingers, etc. One of the leaders, having stepped over one of the brothers as he lay on the ground, touched him with his whip and said :[1]

> Stant ûf durch der reinen martel êre,
> Und hût dich vor der sünden mére.

Thus he went through the whole circle, and whoever had been touched followed him in the same ceremony until all had risen. Now another circle was formed into which the precentors stepped, intoning the second long hymn, while the brothers two by two went around the circle scourging themselves until the blood flowed. In Tilemann's version the song begins thus :

> Tredet herzu, wer bussen welle,
> so flihen wir di heissen helle.
> Lucifer ist bose geselle,
> wen he hat,
> mit beche er in labet.

This was evidently the most important hymn in these bloody exercises. In a more perfect, but still very corrupt form, we have it preserved not only by Closener, but also in a Low German version.[2] Almost the same thoughts and many similar expressions

---

[1] Cf. Closener, p. 107 ff.
[2] Cf. Ph. Wackernagel, Das deutsche Kirchenlied, II 336.

occur in a song of the French Flagellants,[1] which points to the international character of the movement as well as to a common source of the various forms of this hymn. After it had been sung the Flagellants again kneeled down and sang :

> Jhesus wart gelabet mit gallen,
> Des sollen wir an ein cruze fallen. (Tilemann.)

Again they threw themselves on the ground, remaining there for a while until the precentors began :

> Nû hebent ûf die uwern hende,
> das got dis grosze sterben wende.
> Nû hebent ûf die uwern arme,
> das sich got uber uns erbarme.
> Jhêsus, durch diner namen drie,
> Du mach uns, herre, vor sünden frie!
> Jhêsus, durch dîne wunden rôt
> Behüt uns vor dem gehen tôt. (Closener.)

> [1] Or, avant, entre nous tuit frère
> Batons noz charvingues bien fort,
> En remembrant la grant misère
> De Dieu et sa piteuse mort,
> Qui fut pris de la gent amère
> Et vendus et trahi à tort :
> Et battu sa char vierge et clère ;
> Ou nom de ce, batons plus fort.

> Loons Dieu et batons noz pis,
> Et en la doulce remembrance
> De ce que tu feus abeuvrez
> Avec le crueux cop de la lance,
> D'aisil o fiel fut destrampez.
> Alons à genoux par penance ;
> Loons Dieu, vos bras estandez ;
> Et en l'amour de sa souffrance
> Cheons jus en croix à tous lez.

> Batons noz pis, batons no face.
> Tendons noz bras, de grant vouloir
> Dieux qui nous a fait, nous préface
> Et nous doint de cieux le manoir.
> Et gart tous ceulx qu'en ceste place
> En pitié nous viennent veoir
> Jhésus ainsi comme devant.
> —(Leroux de Lincy, Recueil de Chants histor. franc. I 233.)

Then they stretched out their arms in the form of a cross, and beating their breasts, sang:

> Nû slaget uch sère
> durch Cristes êre.
> Dorch Got so lasset di hoffart faren,
> so wel sich Got ober uns irbarmen.

This last song, while not recorded by Closener, is given after Tilemann. It was doubtless used wherever the Flagellants appeared, since it is frequently mentioned by contemporary and later writers. Its Dutch version runs as follows:

> Nu slaet u seer
> door Christus eer
> door God so laet die sonden meer.

An Austrian chronicle (1025-1282), which relates of the earliest Flagellants in 1260, mentions it in the following sentence: Mulieres quoque in domibus simili modo faciendo, et illum cantum psallebant:

> Ir slaht iuch sère
> in cristes êre.
> durch got sô lât die sünde mêre.

Hence it is highly probable that not only parts of songs, but whole hymns, and perhaps even many ceremonies, had been preserved by tradition for nearly a century. With the singing of the hymn just quoted the first part of these dramatic exercises closed. A second and third procession and scourging now followed, during which the continuation of "Tredet herzu, wer bussen welle" was sung.[1] The reading of a long letter which, as they pretended, had

[1] Maria stuont in grossen nöten
Do siu ir liebes kint sach toeten,
Ein swerte ir durch die sele sneit. (Cf. Stabat mater.)
Daz lo dir, sunder, wesen leit.
Des hilf uns lieber herre got,
des biten wir dich durch dinen tot.
   Jhesus riefe in hiemelriche
sinen engeln allen geliche,
er sprach zuo in vil senedeclichen:
die cristenheit wil mir entwichen,
des wil ich lan die welt zergan,
des wissent sicher, one wan.
   dovor behüt uns, herre got,
des bitten wir dich durch dinen tot.

been sent from heaven by Christ, usually closed the services.

Maria bat im sun den süssen :
liebes kint, lo sü dir büssen
so wil ich schicken, daz sü müssen
beseren sich. des bit ich dich,
vil liebes kint, des gewer du mich.
  des bitten wir sunder ouch alle gelich
Welich frowe oder man ire e nuo brechen
daz wil got selber an si rechen :
swebel, bech und ouch die gallen
güsset der tüfel in sie alle.
Furwar sie sint des duvels bot.
  dovor behüt uns, herre got,
  des bitten wir dich durch dinen tot.
Ir mordere, ir strosroubere,
uch ist die rede enteil zuo swere,
ir wellent uch uber nieman erbarn,
des mussent ir in die helle varn.
  dovor behüt uns, herre got,
  des bitten wir dich durch dinen tot.
O we, ir armen wuocherere,
dem lieben got sint ir unmere.
du lihest ein marg al umbe pfunt,
daz zühet dich in der helle grunt,
des bistu iemer me verlorn,
derzuo so bringet dich gottes zorn
  dovor behüt uns, etc.
Die erde erbidemet, sich klübent die steine
ir herten hertzen, ir sullent weinen,
weinent toügen—mit den ougen.
schlahent uch sere—durch Cristes ere.
durch (in) vergiessen wir unser bluot,
daz si uns fur die sünde guot.
  daz hilf uns lieber herre got, etc.
Der den fritag nüt envastet
und den süntag nüt enrastet,
zwar der müsse in der helle pin
eweklich verloren sin.
  dovor behüt uns, etc.
Die e, die ist ein reines leben,
die hat got selber uns gegeben.
ich rat frowen und ir mannen,
daz ir die hochfart lasset dannen.
durch got so laut die hochfart varn,
so wil sich got uber uns erbarn.
  des hilf uns, etc.

Tilemann, finally, has preserved us the first strophes of two hymns which they intoned on leaving the cities and villages:

> O herre vader Jhêsu Christ,
> want du ein herre alleine bist,
> der uns die sunde mach vurgeben,
> un gefriste uns, herre, ûf besser leben,
> das wir beweinen dînen dôt!
> Wir klagen dir, herre alle unse nôt, etc.

Or:

> Ez ging sich unse frauwe, kyrieleison,
> des morgens in dem dauwe, alleluia.
> Gelobet sî Maria!
> Da begente ir ein junge, kyrieleison,
> sîn bart war ime entsprungen, alleluia.
> Gelobet sî Maria! etc.

It was necessary to give a full description of the ceremonies and songs of the Flagellants, in order to illustrate the manner in which Tilemann recorded poetry in his chronicle. Comparing his account with that of Closener and other sources, it will be observed that, although Closener has a more complete text, Tilemann has noted several songs of essential importance for the understanding of the Flagellant movement, which do not occur in Closener. The reason why Tilemann usually does not report more than one strophe of the various hymns is to be found in the fact that they are of interest to him only as newly arisen forms of metrical and musical production. Several times he takes occasion to emphasize that the hymns or " leisen " (kyrieleison), as he calls them, had been composed at this time (der leise ward da gemachet) or belonged exclusively to the Flagellants (ire leisen). Finally, he says: "item du salt wissen, daz dise vurgeschreben leisen alle worden gemachet unde gedicht in der geiselnfart, unde enwas der leisen keine vur gehort." Although Tilemann is mistaken here in regard to the verses "Nu slaget uch sere," which were known as early as 1260, his remark characterizes the manner in which he observed newly arising poetical phenomena. His treatment of these religious hymns will, of course, help to throw light on his account of the remaining popular poetry, as we shall find later. An investigation as to the common source of all the Flagellant poetry is not undertaken in this paper. It is highly probable, however, that it is to be found in Italy, where we meet with the earliest indications of the Flagellant movement in 1260; and that, following the geographical route of the order, it became by translation and tradition the basis of the Flagellant poetry in the various countries.[1]

JULIUS GOEBEL.

[1] A proof for the latter supposition may be found in a passage from a chronicle quoted by Hoffmann, Gesch. des d. Kirchenlieds, p. 132 (Chronicon Pulkavae, Monum. hist. Boem. T. III, p. 232): Eodem anno flagellatorum quaedam secta suboritur, qui velantes capita more claustralium ad cingulum denudati flagellis in estremitatibus nodos habentibus, fortissime se caedebant, quorum etiam quidam processiones, stationes, venias et genuflexiones fecerunt mirabiles, *secundum distinctiones linguarum cantantes.*

[Reprinted from the AMERICAN JOURNAL OF PHILOLOGY, Vol. VIII, No. 4.]

V.—POETRY IN THE LIMBURGER CHRONIK.

II.

The last group of songs preserved by Tilemann seems to have been the most important in the collector's own eyes. It is not only more extensive numerically, but. it is evident that he noted these songs with particular care and pleasure, in several cases not withholding his own criticism : *ein gut lit,* he says (37, 10), *ein gut lit von wise unde von worten* (37, 21). There are about fifteen shorter songs or fragments of such, mostly recorded in the first part of the Chronicle with the events from 1350 to 1380, which seems to indicate that Tilemann himself had witnessed their popularity during his younger days. He has, therefore, either noted them as they arose, or, in case he wrote the Chronicle during the latter part of his life, has in recording them given pleasant reminiscences of his youth. Their prevailing theme is that inexhaustible theme of all popular poetry, love, with but two exceptions, which are didactic in character. The longing for the beloved one, the pain and sorrow of parting, and the promise of faithfulness resound here in such beautiful strains that we may well ask, "How is this possible in an age which marks the decline of German poetry, and which is stirred by movements like that of the Flagellants?" In vain shall we look for a connection with the last representatives of Minnepoetry, whose general character we have already described. Neither will a comparison of the Meistersinger poetry, with its artificial metres and its didactic and allegoric contents, give us a satisfactory answer.[1] There seems to be no doubt that we must look for another source for our songs than those which are historically warranted in German poetry of that time.

We should certainly commit an anachronism were we to treat our chronicler like a literary critic of the present century, equipped with all the methods of historiography. Considering, however, Tilemann's attitude toward poetical phenomena, which we attempted to characterize in our first essay, it is perhaps justifiable to conclude that he himself indicates the source of that kind of poetry

[1] Cf. J. Grimm, Ueber den altdeutschen Meistergesang.

of which he has given us a number of specimens. Certain documents, like the famous passage in Gottfried's Tristan, give evidence of the fact that literary criticism had developed to great perfection in many mediaeval circles. And we can fortunately conceive of a man of fine literary taste in those times without questioning him as to his system of philosophical aesthetics. We may, therefore, at least ask whether it is not strange that Tilemann does not mention one of the popular songs until he has given us the remarkable account of Reinhard von Westerburg and has characterized the poetry of the Flagellants? It would rather be peculiar if such songs had not been sung until the year 1350. But it is quite natural, and entirely within our chronicler's character and the limited, undeveloped means of prose expression, that he thus should have directed the attention of his readers to that kind of poetry which he himself esteemed so highly.

However, even if we do not consider Tilemann's Chronicle one of the first naive attempts at literary criticism or at a history of contemporary German poetry, his book is of great importance for the history of the German "Volkslied," which still remains to be written.[1] The most important effort in this direction, Ludwig Uhland's classical "Abhandlung" (Schriften zur Geschichte und Sage, III), presents the subject from a comparative point of view, and is less concerned with a critical investigation of the historical growth of German popular poetry. Hence Uhland has confined himself almost exclusively to the fifteenth and sixteenth centuries, only occasionally referring to the older forms of the Volkslied in German literature. And in the appendix to his collection (Vol. II 973), where he speaks of his " Quellen" and the linguistic treatment of his text, he simply enumerates and describes the former without making mention of our Chronicle and other important collections; whereas, Tilemann's specimens being the first historical documents of popular poetry after the decline of the " Minnesang," it seems natural that his account should become the starting point of an investigation into the development of the "Volkslied." And while a comparison with the earlier forms of the " Minnesang " and the later " Volkslied " will serve the final aim of this paper, it may perhaps also contribute to a future critical history of German popular poetry.

[1] F. H. Otto Weddigen's Geschichte der deutschen Volkspoesie, a mere compilation without original research, can of course not pass for such.

But before we proceed to such a comparison, a few remarks of a more general character may not be out of place. For although we believe ourselves to have proved that Tilemann himself cannot be the author of the songs recorded by him, it might still be claimed that our songs originated under the influence of the Minnesang. It is one of the principal arguments of Wilmanns that the want of documents of early popular love-poetry is to be explained "aus der Natur des menschlichen Herzens und allmählicher Entwickelung des geistigen Lebens." If through French influence it became gradually known and fashionable in Germany to give artistic expression to the deepest feeling of the human soul, is it not possible that the popular poetry of which our chronicle relates was at least indirectly due to the fact that the German people in general had learned from the Minnepoetry of the court circles and the " Spielleute " to sing their loves ?

K. Burdach, in his essay (Zeitschr. f. d. Alt. XXVII 343 ff.) has, according to my opinion, proved conclusively that we owe this love poetry to the general character of Volkspoesie, which is that of a happy improvisation coming and passing away with the moment of its birth, if we do not possess specimens from the oldest times. He has shown further, by the example of the poetry of many nations, especially of savage tribes, that it is not at all against "die Natur des menschlichen Herzens " to express itself in lyrical strains, perhaps long before the rise of the epos ; and the songs of our chronicle may probably add another argument to the evidence against the fallacious notion of a presumed older age of epic poetry. The defenders of this idea support their opinion mainly by the fact that the exterior world lends itself much sooner and much more easily to an objective artistic treatment by the poet than the world of emotions, and wherever the latter begins to find artistic expression it is supposed to commence with a symbolization of the exterior world, as it is still to be found in the " Natureingang " of the Minnesang and the later Volkslied. I believe this is a prejudice to which even Uhland is somewhat subject, although he says of the poetic form of certain parting songs : "Andre Abschiedslieder entschlagen sich gänzlich der Bilder und Naturanklänge. Das wahre Weh, die innigste Empfindung verschmähen allerdings oft jeden andern Ausdruck als den unmittelbarsten" (Schriften, III 446). But who would deny that "wahres Weh und *innigste Empfindung*," the special characteristic of all true Volkspoesie, should not have found its rhythmical expression at least as early as the exterior world became an object of poetical imagination in epic poetry? It is a psychological fact that the soul, oppressed by violent passions and emotions, loses the freedom necessary for an imaginative artistic treatment of its various conditions. But would we call the rhythmical liberation of the soul, the primitive sounds of deepest emotion that seize us with elementary force, less poetic than the more artistic forms which betray the free play of imagination with the feelings? The almost entire absence of imaginative forms of expressions, of metaphors, Natureingang, etc., in the songs of our chronicle, which is not due to an element of bare reflection, seems to me a proof of their originality and age as well as of the age of the popular love song in general. Even the epic element, pointing to the peculiar circumstances or situation from which the single poem arose, is here wanting. Only in one case Tilemann mentions that the song was composed in praise of a beautiful woman in Strassburg, but, as if perfectly conscious of the individual and general character of popular poetry, he immediately and carefully adds that it was true of *all* good women (unde triffet auch alle gude wibe an, 37, 12).

This simplicity in the expression of feeling, the absence of stylistic qualities peculiar to artistic poetry, may also be observed in most of the few specimens of German popular poetry before the rise of the Minnesong, with which we shall have to compare our songs. To these we count also the German strophes in the Carmina Burana, a collection of Latin " Vagantenpoesie " made in the thirteenth and fourteenth centuries, of both contemporary and of earlier material. Here we only consider those which very probably belong to the twelfth century, and which E. Martin, in his essay on the Carmina Burana (Zeitschr. f. d. Altert. 20, 46 ff.), declared imitations of the Latin poems to which they are appended. Since K. Burdach (Reinmar und Walther, 155 ff.) has refuted Martin's opinion as far as it is based upon metrical considerations, a further discussion of this question is not necessary. Martin, however, in order to support the theory, already advanced by Schmeller, that the German Minnesong had developed from the Latin " Vagantenpoesie," says: " in keiner dieser strophen—so getraue ich mich zu behaupten—ist ein würklich individueller gedanke oder eine hindeutung auf bestimmte verhältnisse zu finden." According to my opinion of the character of the oldest popular love poetry, this seeming defect is rather a strong proof for their age and originality, which is still further strengthened by their metrical qualities, of which we shall treat later. The same artless expression of the deep feeling of love may be found in the following strophe, Car. Bur. 99a:

> Solde ih noh'den tach geleben,
> daç ih wunschen solde
> nah der diu mir froude geben
> mach, ob si noh wolde.
> Min herçe muz nah ir streben;
> möhtih si han holde,
> so wolde ih in wunne sweben,
> swere ih nimmer dolde.

To this I could easily add more specimens of the same character, though varying in their themes, since the joy at the appearance of spring and in its gay dances certainly found also a very early expression in simple improvised strophes.

There is, however, one song among the poems of our chronicle which presupposes a definite situation, and which for this reason, probably, has been inserted in many collections of popular poetry, the " Nonnenlied," 48, 5 :

> Got gebe ime ein vurdreben jar,
> der mich machte zu einer nunnen
> und mir den swarzen mantel gap,
> den wiszen rock darunden.
> Sal ich gewerden eine nunn
> sunder minen willen,
> so wel ich eime knaben jung
> sinen komer stillen.
> Und stillet he mir den minen nit,
> .   daran mach he vurlisen.

The contents of this song immediately remind us of the celebrated Capitulare of Charlemagne, of 789,[1] forbidding the nuns winileodes scribere vel mittere, and seem to prove that winileod may, in this connection, very well mean love-song, though its original meaning, according to Müllenhoff (Z. f. d. A. 9, 128 ff.; MSD. 362 ff.), was probably "Gesellenlied." That these "winileod " were certainly not of a very sacred nature can be seen from the additional clause: et de pallore earum propter sanguinis minuationem. Our song may, therefore, very well be considered a specimen of the poetry of nuns, even should it destroy the modern idea of a mediaeval nun, the creation of sickly romanticists.

---

[1] Cf. Wackernagel, Litgesch. I 4S Anm.; Uhland, Schriften, III 457.

Sappho's classic ἔγω δὲ μόνα κατεύδω was, however, frequently para-
phrased in the nunneries of various centuries.[1]

[1] Since the collections containing this popular poetry are not accessible to
every reader in our country I shall quote some of the songs.
From the sixteenth century we have the following (Böhme, Altdeutsches
Liederbuch, N. 242):

> 1. Ach gott wem sol ichs klagen ♥
>   das herzeleiden mein!
>   Mein Herz will mir verzagen,
>   gefangen muss ich sein;
>   Ins kloster bin ich gezogen
>   in meinen jungen jarn
>   darin ich muste leben
>   kein freud noch luste haben:
>   das klag ich allzeit gott!
> 2. Ach nun zu diser stunde
>   hört was ich sagen tu:
>   *Verflucht seind all mein freunde*
>   die mirs haben bracht darzu!
>   Dass ich mich sol erweren
>   des nicht zu erweren ist,
>   mein gut tun sie verzeren,
>   mein sel höchlich beschweren:
>   das klag ich von himel Christ, etc.

While the former poem reflects the influence of the Reformation to a certain
degree, the following song, from the same century, is entirely composed in the
spirit of "Got gebe im," etc.; cf. Böhme, 243:

> 1. Ich sollt ein nönnlein werden,
>   ich hat kein lust darzu;
>   Ich ess nicht gerne gerste,
>   wach auch nicht gerne fru.
>   Gott geb dem kläffer unglück vil,
>   der mich armes mägdelein
>   ins kloster bringen wil!
> 2. Im kloster, im kloster,
>   da mag ich nicht gesein;
>   Da schneidt man mir mein härlein ab,
>   bringt mir gross schwere pein.
>   Gott geb dem kläffer unglück vil,
>   der mich armes mägdelein
>   ins kloster bringen wil!
> 3. Und wann es komt um mitternacht,
>   schlägt man die glocken an,
>   So hab ich armes mägdelein
>   noch nie kein schlaf getan.

The imperfect rhymes *jar* : *gap* of our song, which are a sign of its age, have induced me to change the first verse of the second strophe in order to establish the rhymes *nunn* : *jung*. All the MSS read here: sal ich ein nunn gewerden ; but it is evident that my proposed reading at least approximates the original text. The rhymes *nunnen* : *drunden, willen* : *stillen*, apparently feminine, are surely to be considered masculine, since none of the last syllables of these words are accented. The expression, *Got gebe ime* ein vurdreben jar, was evidently proverbial and popular ; M. F. 9, 18: *got der gebe in leit!* Walther von der Vogelweide, 119, 17 : *Got gebe ir ēimer guten* tac.

Proceeding to the remaining songs of our chronicle, we find as one of their characteristic features, which they have in common with all true popular poetry, that they are addressed to girls, and not to married women as most poems of the Minnesingers are. This natural, healthy and ethical condition, gradually disclosed again in the course of his development by the classical representative of Minnepoetry, Walther von der Vogelweide, seems to be a matter of course in our poems. And we are surprised at the

> Gott geb dem kläffer unglück vil,
> der mich armes mägdelein
> ins kloster bringen wil!
> 4. Und wann ich vor die äbtissin kom,
> so sicht sie mich sauer an ;
> Vil lieber wolt ich freien
> ein hübschen jungen man,
> Und der mein steter bule mag sein,
> so wär ich armes mägdelein
> des fastens und betens frei.
> 5. Ade, ade, feins klosterlein,
> ade, gehab dich wol !
> Ich weiss ein herzallerliebsten mein,
> der mich erfreuen sol ;
> Auf in setz ich mein zuversicht,
> ein nönnlein werd ich nimmer nicht,
> ade, feins klösterlein !

This song was selected as a specimen of the present time ; cf. Erk, Liederhort, No. 148 :

> 1. O Klosterleben, du Einsamkeit,
> du stilles und ruhiges Leben !
> dir hab ich mich gänzlich ergeben,
> zu führen ein geistliches Leben :
> O Himmel, was hab ich gethan !
> die Liebe war Schuld daran.

sublime simplicity of womanhood which appears in the background, as it were, of these songs. There is no description of the physical beauty of woman, in which the Minnesingers abound; only once the " zarte rote mondelin " is modestly mentioned. All the qualities attributed to her are of a higher ethical character, as *rein*, *gut*, *minneclich*, *zart*, *züchtig*, thus showing the same purity and tenderness of feeling which appears in the earliest German poems addressed to the Virgin Mary. She is the " *liveste frauwe min*," the source of pure "*freude*." There are two strophes which show this very evidently. 65, 2 :

> Gepuret reine und suberlich
> weisz ich ein wip gar minneclich,
> di ist mit zochten wol bewart ;
> ich wolde daz si ez woste, di reine zart.

37, 13 :

> Eins reinen guden. wibes angesichte
> und frauweliche zucht darbi
> di sint werlich gut zu sehen.
> Zu guden wiben han ich plichte,
> wan si sin alles wandels fri.

It is true there are, especially in the earliest Minnesingers, similar expressions of tender feeling, but their poetry was limited

---

2. Des Morgens wenn ich zur Kirche geh,
muss singen und beten alleine ;
und wenn ich das Gloria patri sing,
so liegt mir mein Schätzlein wol immer im Sinn :
O Himmel, was hab ich gethan!
die Liebe war Schuld daran.

3. Dort kommt mein Vater und Mutter her,
sie beten für sich alleine ;
sie haben gar schöne Kleider an,
ich aber muss in der Kutten stahn :
O Himmel, was hab ich gethan!
die Liebe war Schuld daran.

4. Des Mittags wenn ich zum Essen geh,
find ich es mein Tischchen alleine ;
dann ess ich mein Brot und trinke mein Wein :
ach, könnt ich bei meinem schön Schätzchen sein!
O Himmel, was hab ich gethan !
die Liebe war Schuld daran.

5. Des Abends wenn ich nun schlafen geh,
find ich es mein Bettchen alleine ;
dann lieg ich und kann nicht erwarmen :
ach, hätt ich mein Schätzchen in Armen !
O Himmel, was hab ich gethan!
die Liebe war Schuld daran.

to the exclusive circles of the nobility. We cannot prove that their ideas penetrated among the common people, and it is, therefore, almost entirely out of the question that they should have influenced popular poetry. It seems, on the other hand, much more probable that they themselves drew from the same source which flows so refreshingly in the songs of our chronicle. For the first time the ethical spirit of the people, destined to become such a powerful element in the literary regeneration of the eighteenth century, manifests itself independently in these deeply felt songs, and we can follow in the later development of the Volkslied the growth of the human ideal disclosed therein. One of the most important documents for the study of its history can be found in the *Liederbuch* der Clara Hätzlerin (ed. C. Haltaus, 1840), a collection of various kinds of poetry made by a nun of Augsburg in the fifteenth century. Among the 134 lyrical pieces of the first part, which consist of a number of Tagelieder, Meisterlieder, and poems of known poets of that period, we discover several songs of an entirely popular character. Their language and tone resemble so much that of the songs of Tilemann's Chronicle that his assertion of the popularity of his songs cannot possibly be doubted. The monostrophic improvisation of the Limburger songs has developed already into the poem of several strophes in the Lieder-buch of the fifteenth century, and the purity and depth of their feeling mark a striking contrast to the lascivious tone of the Tage-lieder which immediately precede them. They also are addressed to girls, who are called *schön, frumm, wandelsfrey* (No. 31, 1), *die rain, die säuberlich* (pretty) (38, 8), *zart lieb* (48, 2), etc. They are *der höchste schatz* und *gröste fräd* (65, 1), their heart is *genaden vol*, etc. It is unnecessary to add that woman is described with the same colors in the classical popular songs of the sixteenth century.

This pure and high conception of womanhood could certainly not be without influence upon the relation of man to woman, and it is here that the ethical spirit of true popular poetry reveals itself in a sublime manner. The final aim for which all the "service" of the Minnesinger was intended is never mentioned in these songs. Instead of the desire for possession, or of sensual enjoyment, it is the idea of eternal fidelity which rules the feelings of all these songs, and it is perhaps significant that the theme of infidelity is scarcely treated in the earliest folksongs. In the following songs this plea for fidelity appears as simply and tenderly expressed as anywhere in the realms of poetry. 37, 23:

Ach reinez wip von guder art,
gedenke an alle stedicheit,
daz man auch ni von dir gesait,
daz reinen wiben obel steit.
Daran saltu gedenken
und salt nit von mir wenken,
di wile daz ich daz leben han.
Noch ist mir einer klage not
von der livesten frauwen min,
daz ir zartez mondelin rot
wel mir ungenedig sin.
Si wil mich zu grunt vurderben,
untrost wel si an mich erben,
dazu enweisz ich keinen rat.

53, 17 :

Ich wel in hoffen leben vort, ·
ob mir it heiles moge geschehen
von der livesten frauwen min.
Spreche si zu mir ein fruntlich wort,
so solde truren von mir flihen.

Respons. { Ich wel in hoffen leben vort,
ob mir it heiles moge geschehen
von der livesten frauwen min.
Ir gunste i mit heile bekorte.
Ach Got, daz ich si solde sehen.

Respons. { Ich wel in hoffen leben vort
ob mir it heiles moge geschehen
von der livesten frauwen min.

65, 20 :

Wie mochte mir umber basz gesin
in ruwen?
Ez grunet mir in dem herzen min
als uf der auwen.
Daran gedenke
Min lip, und nit enwenke.

Of all the songs recorded by Tilemann, 37, 23 will probably
remind us most of the style of the Minnesongs, especially since it
is mentioned as early as 1350. A closer examination of its
language, however, will show its relation to earlier and later folksongs: *von guder art;* cf. Goedeke, Liederbuch aus dem 16 Jahr-
hundert, No. 14, 1 : *von edler art;* 72, 16 : *von edler art. stedicheit*
is the technical term for fidelity in the Minnesongs as well as in the
earlier folksongs; cf. MF. 16, 1 ; Walther v. d. Vogelw. 43, 29 :
wir man wir wellen daz diu staetekeit in guoten wiben gar ein
krône sî; Liederbuch der Hätzlerin, 36, 17 ; 72, 31 ; 117, 10. In
one of the fragments of our chronicle which probably notes only

the beginnings of three strophes, the word *truwe* is used; cf. 56, 18, ich wil dir i mit ganzen truwen leben. The *mondelin rot* occurs in one of the oldest strophes of the Car. Bur. as *roservarwer mund* (136a). *wenken* is very often used in the Liederb. d. H. *di wile daz ich daz leben han;* cf. M. F. 9, 25: die wile unz ich daz leben hân.

53, 17 is of great interest in regard to strophic construction, *in hoffen leben;* cf. L. d. Hätzl. 102, 31, *in hoffen ich leb;* and our chronicle 49, 11, *hoffen heldet mir das leben.*

65, 20 must certainly be called the gem of Tilemann's collection. "*Wi mochte mir umber basz gesin*" is a proverbial expression; cf. Parcival, 222, 30, *wie möhte der imer baz gesin.* L. d. H. Sprüche, No. 49, *Ich bin ir sy mein, wie möcht uns baiden bas gesein. Ez grunet mir in dem herzen min* occurs in the mystics; cf. Pfeifer, Deutsche Mystiker, I 4, dar leben unses herren dar *grunete* und wuchs in der lûte herze; cf. MSH. 112b, so *grunet* mîn herze, als iuwer klê.

The idea of fidelity expresses itself most beautifully also in the two little parting songs of Tilemann's collection. The pain of parting was very effectively introduced into the Tagelieder by the Minnesingers in order to form a strong contrast to the feeling of happiest enjoyment to which the lovers had previously given themselves up (cf. Walter De Gruyter, Das deutsche Tagelied, 37 ff.) The situation as well as the tone of expressing the sorrow of parting is entirely different in our songs, and perfectly in accordance with their ethical character. 45, 5 :

> Ach Got, daz ich si miden musz,
> di ich zu den freuden hatte irkoren,
> daz dut mir werlich alzu we.
> Mochte mir noch werden ein fruntlich grusz,
> des ich so lange han enboren.

51, 22 :

> Miden scheiden,
> daz dut werlich we
> uzer maszen we.
> Und enist daz nit unmoeglichen,
> von einer di ich gerne anse.

My reasons for arranging the last song in this manner will be given later. I believe it is a whole strophe and does not contain the beginnings of several strophes, as Lorenz and Wyss seem to think. Several expressions in both songs recur almost verbally in numerous parting songs not only of the sixteenth century, but also in the Minnesingers and in popular poetry of the present time (cf.

Wilmanns, Leben Walthers, 399). The intimate relation of these songs of the Limburger Chronik to those of the Liederbuch der Hätzlerin appears most manifestly in the following poems quoted from the latter. 50:

Gesegen dich got, liebs fräwlin zart!
Ich schaid von dir vnd lasz dich hie,
Vergisz mein nit, et leyt mir hart,
Wann ich dir was mit triuen ye
Vnd will dir wencken nymmermer.

Gesegen dich got, mein hertz ist dein,
Du bist mein trost, mein vsserwelt!
Die weil ich leb, so will ich sein
Mit stättigkeit zu dir geselt!
So volgt nur fräd, wä ich hin cher.

Seid hoffen ist für trauren gůt,
So hoff ich wäger werd mein sach.
Ye lieber chind, ye scherpffer růt,
Halt vest, als mir dem gnad versprach,
So hab ich fräd on wider ker.

Gesegen dich got, ist nit mein fůg,
Es pringt mir leid vnd senende clag.
Meiner tusend trügen laids genuog
An dem, das ich allaine trag;
Doch nert mich hoffen wider her.

77:

Ach schaiden, du vil senende not,
Das mir dein gwalt ye gepott,
Du machst mich plaich, rott,
Bis in den tot,
Das mir nit würser mag gesein.

Das hertz ist allzeit traurens vol,
Wann sich lieb von lieb schaiden sol;
Es tůt nit wol!
Darumb ich dol
Gar senlich in dem hertzen mein.

Mit manigem seüftzen ynneclich
Ständ swär mein gedenck hinder sich,
Wie wol ich
Gen nyemantz sprich,
Dest geringer ist das hertz nicht.

86:

Meiden hat mich ser verwundt
Gar tieff in meines hertzen grunt;
Das macht ir lieb, von der mir kunt
Ist worden gantze stättikait.

Nun hilff gelück zu stätter triw,
Wann meiden pringt gross affterrew,
Gen ainer da mein lieb ist new
Tag vnd nacht on vnderschaid.

Sy liebt mir ye für all dis welt,
Ich hoff, ich vind des widergelt,
Das vnser lieb bleib vnvermelt ;
In praun vnd grön ist sy geclaidt.

A decisive proof for the age of our songs, and consequently
also indirectly for the age of German Volkspoesie in general, may,
according to my opinion, be gathered from their metrical construction. And we shall find that in the structure of the verses as well
as of the strophes they follow old Germanic metrical laws.

For centuries German prosody was suffering under the ascendancy
of rules abstracted from the ancients, and even classic poets of the
last century were mainly guided by their metrical instinct and feeling.
The liberation of those ancient fetters we owe to the excellent researches of R. Westphal, who for the first time showed conclusively
that the principle of accent and rhythm, and not that of quantity,
is the fundamental metrical law of German poetry (Theorie der
Neuhochdeutschen Metrik, 2 Aufl., 1877). In his essay, Zur ver-
gleichenden Metrik der indogermanischen Völker (Kuhn's Zeitschr. IX 437), he had made the revolutionizing discovery of the
common basis of all Indogermanic prosody consisting of 2 X 8
syllables divided by a caesura after the eighth syllable. In the
second edition of Die Metrik der Griechen von A. Rossbach und
R. Westphal, 1868, he attempted to show that the same principle
of metrical construction was to be found in the anushtubh of the
Veda and the çloka of classical Sanskrit, as well as in the versus
saturnius and the old German "Langzeile." His opinion was
supported in regard to the prosody of the Avesta by K. Geldner,
in his treatise, Ueber die Metrik der jüngeren Avesta, Tübingen,
1877. Starting from the results obtained by these two scholars,
Professor F. Allen (Kuhn's Zeitschr. XXIV 556 ff.) found that
the metrical unity of the Indogermanic verse was the tetrapodic
hemistich, out of which the Indian and old Germanic versus
longus and also the Greek hexameter had gradually developed.
Independently of Allen, H. Usener, in his excellent book, Alt-
griechischer Versbau, ein Versuch vergleichender Metrik, Bonn,
1887, which also abounds in valuable suggestions for German

metrics, has reached the same results.[1] In order to support his theory of the development of the hexameter from the tetrapodic Indogermanic "Urvers," Usener justly points to the fact: von hause aus gibt es nur éinen deutschen vers von vier hebungen. Er wird nicht gemessen nach silbenzahl, nicht nach quantität, sondern nach jenen vier hebungen, die vom sprachlichen hochton getragen sind. Das ist die form aller unserer erzählenden poesie gewesen, so weit wir sie zurück verfolgen können und ebenso der *volksmässigen* lyrik bis auf den heutigen tag. In the course of his discussion he calls attention to the principal peculiarities of the prosody of German popular poetry which are mostly due to the influence of rhythm, as already observed by E. Stolte in his Metrische Studien über das deutsche Volkslied, 1883, and recently treated by E. Sievers in his essay, Die Entstehung des deutschen Reimverses (Paul & Braune's Beitrage, XIII 121 ff.)[2]

While we find in the development of the artistic Minnepoetry a gradual observance of the regular change of arsis (Hebung) and thesis (Senkung), the entire omission as well as the accumulation of a number of theses between two arses will be frequently noticed in popular poetry. It is wrong to see in the omission of the thesis the effect of a conscious artistic reflection on the part of the poet, as it has been done by Bartsch,[3] who discovered it in the Nibelungenlied, and by R. Becker,[4] who believes to be able to prove it in the earliest Austrian Minnesongs. The absence of the thesis is to be explained not only " aus der freude an kraftvoller betonung " (Usener), but also by the dipodic structure of the German verse, and the consequent distinction of a " haupt- und nebenton."

A mere glance at the songs of our chronicle will convince us that we have here before us the old Germanic verse of four accents with a frequent syncope of the thesis. I have noticed the following cases : 37, 31 von der livestén fraúwen mín; 37, 32 daz ir zártez móndelín rót; 37, 33 wel mir úngenédig sín; 48, 10 sunder mínén wíllen; 48, 12 sinen kómér stillen; 53, 19 von der livestén fraúwen mín; 65, 21 in rúwén; 65, 23 als uf der aúwén. A similar syncope of the thesis may be observed in the following German strophes of the Carm. Bur.: 99a, 5; 100a, 5; 127a, 4; 129a;

[1] Cf. R. Westphal, Gött. gel. Anz., No. 20, 1887.
[2] Unfortunately, I did not receive Professor Wilmanns' exceedingly profound treatise, Der altdeutsche Reimvers, until this essay was printed.
[3] Cf. Bartsch, Untersuch. über das Nibelungenlied, 142 ff.
[4] R. Becker, Der altheimische Minnesang, 50 ff.

141a, 3; for it is absurd, according to my opinion, if Martin adopts in these cases "sprachlich unrichtige Betonung " in order to save his theory (cf. Burdach, Reinmar und Walther, 156). By the aid of these observations concerning accentuation, I believe to be able to reconstruct one of our songs hitherto considered as a fragment, and as a proof for the fact that Tilemann noted the melody rather than the text of the songs as he did in the case of the Flagellant poetry (cf. Lorenz, Deutschlands Geschichtsquellen ' I 144). I propose to read 51, 22 in the following manner:

> Mídén, scheídén
> dáz dut wérlich wé
> úszer mászen wé.
> und eníst daz nít unmoéglichén,
> von eíner, dí ich gérn ansé.

A similar difference between the songs of our chronicle and the artistic Minnepoetry is to be found in regard to the use of the anakrusis. The strict rules of prosody of the Minnepoetry allow only monosyllabic anakrusis, and there are only a few exceptions to this rule even in the beginnings of the artistic poetry (cf. Haupt, M. F. 292). The popular poetry, however, has always treated this rule with disrespect. While the exceptions in M. F. show only dissyllabic anakrusis, most of the cases occurring in Spervogel and other poems of a popular nature, an anakrusis of two, three and more syllables is not unusual in our songs : 37, 31 von der livestén; 37, 32 daz ir zártez; 65, 23 als uf der aúwén; 37, 13 eins reinen gúden. The same treatment of the anakrusis prevails in Car. Bur. 112; 106a, 7; 108a, 4.

A further proof for the popularity and age of the songs of our chronicle can be obtained from an observation of the nature of the rhymes. Although the distinction between masculine and feminine rhymes appears quite plainly in our songs, the masculine rhyme is preferred in most cases, a peculiarity also of the Car. Bur.: 106a, 107a, 115a, 129a, 133a, 134a. Imperfect rhyme, quite rarely occurring in artistic poetry after 1190, may be observed in the following cases: 37, 4 *laszen* (lân) *enkan;* 37, 23 *art* : *sait;* 48, 6 *nunnen* : *darunden* (darunnen?); 48, 9 *nunn*:*jung*; 53, 18 *geschehen* :*flihen.* The fact that even the unaccented *e* can bear the rhyme, as e. g. in 65, 21, is entirely in harmony with the rhythmical laws of German popular poetry, which frequently allow a strong accent on weak syllables.

Still more important proof for the age of our songs may be obtained by observations from the structure of the strophes. It is certainly true that Tilemann's attention was principally directed to the "wise," i. e. the musical melody of the songs he recorded. The following remark will, however, show that the words and their strophic structure did not escape his notice. He says in the year 1360: "Item in disem selben jare vurwandelten sich dictamina unde gedichte in Duschen lidern. Want man bit her lider lange gesongen hat mit funf oder ses gesetzen, da machent di meister nu lider die heissent widersenge, mit dren gesetzen. Auch hat ez sich also vurwandelt mit den pifen unde pifenspel unde hat ufgestegen in der museken, unde ni also gut waren bit her, als nu in ist anegangen. Dan wer vur funf oder ses jaren ein gut pifer was geheissen in dam ganzen lande, der endauc itzunt nit eine flige." Is it not strange that Tilemann, who noticed this change so carefully, should not have preserved us at least one of those songs of five or six strophes which in that year became unfashionable? With but three exceptions the recorded songs consist of one strophe only, and a comparison of one of those exceptions (53, 17), called by him a "lit unde widergesenge," with the Meisterlieder accessible to me [1] disclosed no relation whatever. The simple answer to our question will therefore be that it is the old monostrophic form of the popular German song which we have here before us, a form which is given by the improvisatory nature of this kind of poetry.[2] The same form is found in the Car. Bur. and the oldest specimens of the Minnesong, so that it is quite safe to say that all the old German love poetry of which we have no documents consisted of monostrophic poems. The entire absence of songs of five and six strophes can be taken as another proof that Tilemann consciously distinguished between Meisterlieder and that poetry which he recorded.

It is a well known fact that the old Germanic "Urvers" of four accents, twice or four times repeated, constituted the old Germanic "Urstrophe" as it appears e. g. in Otfrid. Among the songs of our chronicle we meet this strophe twice, 65, 2, and in the "Nonnenlied," 48, 5. There are, however, several songs composed in a strophe which differs very much from this old and simple form. Comparing it with other known strophes we might be inclined to

---

[1] K. Bartsch, Meisterlieder der Kolmarer Handschrift; Goedeke-Tittmann, Liederbuch.
[2] Cf. Scherer, Deutsche Studien, I 333; Burdach, ibid. 165.

declare it a variety of the old popular Moroltstrophe, but a more careful inspection will show this to be impossible. According to Scherer's investigations, based upon the theories of Müllenhoff (Zeitschrift für d. Altertum, XVII 569 ff., and Deutsche Studien, I 283 ff.), the Moroltstrophe developed from the old custom of lengthening the last of the four verses constituting the old German strophe. The first half of this " Langvers," separated from the latter part by a caesura, was inserted as a new verse in the strophe, and, since it does not rhyme with any of the other verses, is called " Waise." As a further peculiarity of strophes containing a " Waise," Scherer pointed out that a monosyllabic (stumpfe) Waise will always appear between feminine rhymes and a dissyllabic (klingende) Waise between masculine rhymes. Since a Waise may be placed before any one of the four·verses of the original strophe, we get strophes of five, six, seven and eight verses. In my opinion Müllenhoff-Scherer's theory of the development of the " Waise " is somewhat mechanical, and, for various reasons, principally musical ones, I believe that the Waise is a separate verse introduced into the strophe of four verses after an old German custom.[1] Yet, whether we accept Scherer's theory or not, we will not be able to explain the strophe of the Limburger songs by the Moroltstrophe. The usual form of the latter is :

```
4 — masc. a
4 — masc. a
4 — masc. b
4 ∪ fem.   c (Waise)
4 — masc. b
```

of which there are several varieties, all agreeing, however, in having the Waise immediately before the last verse. The form of the strophe of three songs in our chronicle, on the contrary, is :

```
4 ∪ fem.  a              or, 4 — masc. a
4 — masc. b                  4 ∪ fem.  b
3 ∪ fem.  c (Waise)          4 — masc. c (Waise)
4 ∪ fem.  a                  4 — masc. a
4 — masc. b                  4 ∪ fem.  b.
```

It can easily be seen that this strophe has none of the peculiarities of the Moroltstrophe : the position of the Waise before the last verse and the distinction of masculine rhyme and dissyllabic

[1] Cf. R. Becker, ibid. 42 ; but also R. M. Meyer, Grundlagen des Mittelhochdeutschen Strophenbaus.

Waise. We find, however, in all the songs composed after this
form a strong pause after the third verse, the close of the first sentence even typographically indicated by a period. Among all the
strophes of the old popular poetry I found a similar form only in
the very old strophe of the Car. Bur. :

> nah mine gesellen ist mir we.
> Gruonet der walt allenthalben :
> wa ist min geselle 'alselange '?
> Der ist geriten hinnen,
> owi, wer sol mich minnen?

Richard M. Meyer, in his exceedingly interesting and suggestive
treatise quoted above (Grundlagen des Mhd. Strophenbaus, 79),
has pointed to the fact that in two old songs preserved under the
name of Dietmar von Eist, 37, 4 ; 37, 18, a similar pause may be
noticed. He further compares M. F. 3, 7; 3, 12, and several of
Neidhard's popular songs, and finds in the form a, a, b | , a
reminiscence of the Ljópaháttr of the Edda, as he sees in the old
Otfridstrophe a reminiscence of the Kvipuháttr. I believe that
the first three verses of our songs in question have preserved the
same reminiscence of the Ljópaháttr. And although the position
of the rhymes in our songs is more artistic than that in the Otfridstrophe (a, a, b, b), I think that their more artistic arrangement is
a device to bridge over the pause after the third verse. Should
the Moroltstrophe, as Meyer supposes, also have arisen from the
Ljópaháttr, then the form of our strophe would still be a highly
interesting and peculiar document for the transition of alliterative
into rhymed poetry.

An excellent illustration of this process may probably be found
in the strophic structure of 53, 17. The repetition of the first
three verses in the responsorium will at least show that the form
a, a, b was still felt as a strophic whole, while the alliterations: *hoffen*,
heiles, *frauwen*, *fruntlich*, *flihen*, etc., are additional reminiscences
of its antiquity. In the later development of German popular
lyrics this form is dropped almost entirely ; only once have I found
it, in the Ambraser Liederbuch, No. 81. The question, however,
has frequently occurred to me whether the tripartite form of the
various strophic structures of the Minnesingers has not developed
more organically from the Limburger strophe than from the
Moroltstrophe.

Summing up the results of these investigations, I believe we are
justified in drawing the following conclusions:

The singular position of the Limburger Chronik in the literature of the fourteenth century, and its great value for the history of German literature in general, are principally due to its author's interest for the poetical phenomena of his time.. While he faithfully recorded important facts concerning the Minnesong and religious poetry, his greatest merit consists in the preservation of contemporary specimens of popular songs which cannot be classed with any of the existing forms of artistic poetry. We must therefore consider them as documents of a popular poetry which developed by the side of the poetry historically known to us. A careful comparison of its contents and form with that of earlier and later popular poetry makes it highly probable that German folksongs have existed since the oldest times, although we do not possess documents for all the various periods of its history. The language and the metrical structure of the Limburger songs furnish especially strong proofs of the antiquity of popular German love-poetry. The songs of the Limburger Chronik are therefore very important documents for throwing light upon the character and development of the earlier as well as of the later German Volkslied.[1]

JULIUS GOEBEL.

[1] It is gratifying to me to find that Edward Schröder, the able editor of Scherer's Literaturgeschichte, in an essay on Die erste Kürenbergerstrophe (Zeitschr. f. d. Alt. XXXII, 1 Heft, 137 ff.) has reached the same results regarding the importance of the Limburger songs for the study of the older German lyrics. The strophe which Schröder compares with the first Kürenbergersong in order to reconstruct the text of the latter was excluded from my discussion on account of its didactic nature. Its metrical form is, however, a variety of the same which we find in 37, 13; 45, 5; 53, 17, and which I have attempted to explain, p. 464 ff.